ILLUMINATE ME

Poetry for Life's Uncertainties

ILLUMINATE ME

Poetry for Life's Uncertainties

Hannah Grace Spenner

To the people who hear me, and to
those navigating life's uncertainties.

Embracing another's words carries a fine luminescence, for it allows us to see the world through their perspective. In that connection, the act of listening and understanding becomes just as transformative as crafting our own stories, shaping us in ways we never anticipated.

1 content warning
2 hold close
3 primrose path
4 suppression
5 traveling emotions
7 be honest
8 dear procrastination
9 vagabond
10 void
11 daydream
12 lest I wake
13 midnight smoke in solitude
14 hold my echoes
15 ink that stains
16 conversation starter
17 no rest for chaos
18 deep-rooted sorrow
19 whispers of the wind
20 deceptions of vibrancy
21 whirlwinds of womanhood
22 abuse of power
23 twenty-three
24 silent witness
25 obscurity island
26 new perception
27 healing spell
28 living in fear
29 cycles
30 the story of hands
31 drunk on you

32 grow with me
33 jamais vu
34 never cease
35 fire starter and the wolf
36 sister suicide
37 ask me why
38 us four
40 infinite second
41 sleep paralysis
42 chemical confessions
43 escaping love
44 gaslit
45 point-blank
46 opportunity cost
47 please
48 seize permission
49 karmic chaos
50 to the friends who knew me well
51 abandoning self
52 congruency
53 paranoid past
54 inward
55 haikyou
56 protective parallels
57 purple skies
58 romanticizing
59 steadfast pillar
60 demons
61 weep for the weak
62 abysmal

63 writer's requiem
64 coulda woulda shoulda
65 clatter and gold
66 coping
67 intoxicate me
68 authentication
69 the overthink
70 enmeshing
71 words wrung
72 unspoken paranoia
73 wise or foolish
74 foster kid
75 palpitate
76 enfolding thoughts
77 lies within my bones
78 golden
79 our thing
80 perfume
81 insomnia
82 backwash
83 transitioning thoughts
84 darkness dies
85 anxiety attack
86 day one
87 path to forgiveness
88 plateau
89 composure
90 catastrophically different
91 blessed be
92 summarizing life beyond addition

93 watching me
94 disarray
95 be that cliché
96 the fawning
97 unbind
98 non-apology
99 mother's hymn
100 removing dysfunction
101 dust reveals
102 turning the page
103 anti-poem
104 count and erase
105 evaluate your standards
106 epilogue
107 reminded
108 virtual unstring
109 odyssey
110 delusion
111 leave me speechless
112 under the skin
113 entangled
114 too complex
115 in the cosmos
117 oblivion
118 change my mind
120 the plethora
121 bidding farewell
123 poppin'
124 drown or break
126 fables

127 stressor
128 trusting
129 meant to be
130 be your own
131 infatuated
132 transpiring
133 the unraveling
134 settling for more
135 extremes
136 dawning
137 free to be
138 premonition
139 shape
140 river of wishes
141 vali-date with self
142 second thoughts
143 quiet flirtation
144 repeating
145 heather
146 gentle rage
147 not just the man
148 sea me
149 fly on the wall
150 savage
151 i forgive you
152 the night I fell for you
153 define them
154 shadow self
155 prudent
156 faltering

157 landescape
158 pores
159 intent
160 mother's lesson
161 moths are only temporary
162 treat me
163 dark empath
164 the test
165 that man
166 my father's instilled words
167 psycho
168 baggage
169 veracity
170 take the risk
171 pacific northwest
172 overwater
173 spilling
174 deepest entirety
175 milestones of self-honesty
176 metamorphosis
178 kill them
179 dweller
180 trust the journey
181 untapped
182 practice and patience
183 ethos
184 to build value
185 companion
186 we are in a battle between
187 illuminate me

ILLUMINATE ME

Poetry for Life's Uncertainties

CONTENT WARNING

Dear Reader,

Before you embark on this journey through the pages of my book, I wish to inform you about the nature of its contents. This book delves into topics that are both complex and sensitive. It includes depictions of death, suicide, trauma, abuse, nightmarish imagery, drug use, mental health, foul language, boundaries, and violence, among other challenging or dark themes. These subjects are handled with the intent to bring awareness, understanding, and empathy, but I recognize that they can be deeply triggering for some individuals. I believe in the power of sharing stories to explore difficult and often unspoken aspects of the human experience, but I also want to prioritize the well-being of my readers. If you find yourself impacted by these topics, I encourage you to seek support if needed. Please consider this information carefully before deciding to read further and do so at your discretion.

With respect from the author,

hannah grace spenner

HOLD CLOSE

Of course, love has conditions—

because to love means to sacrifice self, and we must place circumstantial order to how we feel. Too much, and we forget who we are meant to be as individuals. Too little, and we risk living an arrogant life.

Hold close your sense of self
and the boundaries that define you.

Hold close the ones you love, because they help shape you.

Hold close the value of your conditions, and respect theirs.

PRIMROSE PATH

Upon my path, the dust settles in slight,
where daffodils charm roads I choose to tread.
In the aftermath, friendly thoughts take flight,
though blind in sight, my inner vision's fed.
A blurred veil masks the paths that lay ahead.

I walk this way, the day turns into night.
My primrose path, now bare of floral bed.
The ticking hands devour time's brief might.
Their pleasures once so clear, now turn to dread.
In showers, their essence will gently spread.

Yet daffodils, ever golden in sight,
set firm against the paths I've come to shun.
They lead me not to stray but to the light,
where the choice to wander becomes a run.
Daffodils grow over primrose, in spite.

SUPPRESSION

There's a line we arrange between
what we silence and everything.
Some are made of rocks
and some are purely string.
If we choose to observe closer
we will find that those lines,
aren't anything beyond
concealed warning signs.
These lethargic lines
question the interpretable.
By suppressing our voices
the world becomes unreachable.
Listen to the silence;
it demands to be heard.
Yet open our mouths,
they call for a word.
What is the objective
after each case adjourned?
The time to speak
is rightfully earned!
So many unspoken lessons
living life as a screenplay.
There's a time when the mind
is where the words should stay.
But the moment that emotion
is stronger than muscle,
there is absolutely no reason
for words to be muffled.

TRAVELING EMOTIONS

I sat alone with Delay,
and a voice so slow—
she spoke simply of play.
I found that her day
ended with the birth of a crow.

I ran with Arrogance.
Her words shook the air.
No thought to my intelligence,
for her ears gave no chance.
They were molded of stoneware.

I smiled with Happiness.
Her face, so light that the sun
even squinted at her brightness.
I offered a hand to this priestess,
and she chanted the songs unsung.

I cried with Sorrow.
There wasn't any room for talks
as she handed me air to borrow.
Weight of it all decided to grow,
and we felt heavy under the rocks.

(continued)

(continued)

I glared with Hate.
As a dark haze stole lucidity,
she said this is my fate,
if I reach for the bait
that disguised itself as validity.

I concealed with Fear.
Holding each other's hearts as our own,
shadows inched toward a dripping tear.
Then did I realize it was a hazy mirror
that reminded me that I was all alone.

I lay with Love.
It wasn't her words that blinded,
but the intent of her actions above.
All that she had done, thereof;
Both the heart and the mind were ignited.

BE HONEST

The skin carries stories from wars, surpassed.
Mindsets repeat through generations and we
seek refuge within. Our eyes read the histories,
yet evolution seeps from our mouths. These
horror sounds teach me that my worth is less
than yours. I am the color that others say ____.
All on Earth is stained from the blood of our
ancestors who traveled from elsewhere!
Fighting and striving to change the stars for
themselves, their roots, and those they love.
We all stand in the fragments of what all
humankind has created out of colors—
pointing and shouting: *We are one of the same!*
Echoes mimic the cry for freedom, and we all
continue to live our lives divided; taking for granted
what all of our ancestors really fought for: an honest life.

DEAR PROCRASTINATION

We need a break. You are suffocating me with your bullshit excuses and your constant need for attention. You pull from the very essence of who I am. I give you power only for you to provide me with no reward, friendship, or respect. You continue to take advantage of my kindness and then expect me to thank you. I have boundaries and standards; however, you continue to rip my opportunities away from me due to your lack of confidence. You are so afraid to be alone. I see what you're trying to do. You think that turning me into a hypocrite and a coward will cause me to depend on you. You want me to go to you when things get stressful. I want to reach a better version of myself, but I can't do that with you hindering my ability to think correctly. I must take a stand. I don't want you to visit me anymore. I know that I have so much more potential than your limitations.

You drain the life out of me. I want to see things in a clear light, but when I'm with you, all I feel is exhausted and depressed. Instead of building upon my skills and passions, you utilize my time with frivolous things. I'm not sorry anymore—you're a liar and a cheater. I cannot allow this relationship to drag me down into the depths of repetition. You cause me to despise myself. Although I used to be very inviting of your relaxed authority, you made me ravenous for the easy paths in life. This brings no true happiness or challenge required for personal progress. I need my determination and discipline back. You offer nothing of the sort. You have no control over me anymore. Nonetheless, I've met someone new… *Growth.*

VAGABOND

A mediocre vagabond.
Where are my people?
I roam like a desolate spirit.
Reaching,
teaching
myself the ins and outs
of emotional intelligence.
Who am I to say I can end my pursuit?
I hear the singular voice in my mind,
and she whispers that she feels distant
in a crowded room.

VOID

Some people are afraid of the
things that sleep inside of them;
the perilous part that lies dormant
in the crevices of their deeper thoughts:
we all have the void.

DAYDREAM

Fictitious shapes dance before my lids.
The voices toss and turn their bids.
Joyous passion pulses within the air.
My fingertips press against my ear.
A journey through a gleaming world.
Trepidation is absent, and dreams twirl.
Illumination radiates courage to speak.
I open my mouth to descend a shriek!
A silence moves across the space,
as each eye stops and sees my face.
Forming ambition as I step forward.
Words escape this dream unheard of.

LEST I WAKE

My silence comes from the part of me
that tells me I'm stronger than all this mayhem.
That very part also declares that it's okay to feel silenced,
lest I wake the resting beast hibernating in the mouths of others.

MIDNIGHT SMOKE IN SOLITUDE

An existential comatose lifts me from this very force of consciousness. I think about the way my external self is controlled by the reign. As I hear the rain trickling down the side of the apartment building, I am urged to believe that my story may be written about me, and not by me. Our memories are made up of temporal lobe exhaustion and our short past filled with sticky notes left over from yesterday; archaic, like the dates scribbled on the covers of my planners. I am a maiden in the eyes of the goddess—yet a woman in the eyes of a man. Shall I lift my pen in the morning, while the birds feed their young? Or, perhaps, the evening when the moon has barely begun. It is said that my words write my story, but it seems that others write the reports. Till then, I will lie here, wondering who my author is in hopes of asking the questions unanswered.

HOLD MY ECHOES

Hear me when I tell you all
the things that I find dear.
Listen to the way my voice echoes
through the waves of sound.
The words rock like a ship lost at sea,
and you see defiance.
I am searching for my way in this world
full of drowning spirits.
This ship leaks, and I am soaked in the belief
that I am too lost to be found.
You place the weight of your words on me
when I already carry my own.
My language searches for yours
through the crashing surges.
Your verses are foreign from land that
establishes authority over peace.
Look into my eyes and say they
have not lived through the same hurricane.
Analyze the space between my words and
find yourself learning my language.
Reach out to me,
hold my echoes,
and we can understand why we feel lost at sea.

INK THAT STAINS

Writing words within my veins;
the blood is black—the ink that stains.
Words are wolves; they fashion a grin.
Always devouring me under sheepskin.
Dripping, dripping—the words spill out.
I'm drowning the page before me, no doubt.
Into the world, they creep, and they crawl.
Mindlessly my hand begins to scrawl.

CONVERSATION STARTER

Forced to speak to a stranger before me
while the awkward silence lingers like
the stench of conventional social normality—

"How is your day as a woman in America?"
"Does your favorite color match all of ours?"
"Do you listen to rap or rock or country?"
"Are you a satanist? I see you like stars."

Don't shape your views by the outer shell you see,
for you've felt the weight of judgment's gaze.
Your words paint me as an outsider, a mere child.
If only you could walk in my shoes, understand my days.

Inquire about my aspirations, where I see myself in five years,
or the reasons behind my choice of Doc Marten boots.
Let's move beyond these trivial queries,
seek to know me, my essence, my roots.

NO REST FOR CHAOS

Cry out with a voice that echoes in the night,
with words that are born from shadows and blight.
Through nights filled with doubt, in solitude's cast,
speak truths that emerge from whispers of the past.

Oh, Sister so young, with a spirit so fierce!
In a world where the meek fates often pierce.
Become the huntress, with courage unbound;
never yielding to those who circle around.

From deep within, let your light fiercely burn.
Oh Sister, with passion, let them discern!
In minds that seek knowledge, find strength untold.
Grasp the immortal, be fearless and bold.

Sense the world's rhythm, its unending dance.
Live out your journey, give dreams a chance.
Sister, with feelings, let your voice be heard!
Unsilence your battle with every word.

Stand firm, with ancestors' strength in your veins.
Resist those who'd bind you with invisible chains.
Conformity's path leads but to regret...
Sister, in chaos, forgive but never forget!

DEEP-ROOTED SORROW

My tears spill from my face,
watering the tree that keeps
my feet rooted to the ground.

The splashing of waterworks
has me bound to the sensation
of being drowned, once again.

WHISPERS OF THE WIND

A whisper floated on the wind,
telling me I have not sinned.
Yet the voice within lulled words
that stripped away truth; untrimmed.
The validity that quakes the cage:
parts of me unshared shakes with rage.
To determine the lie stapled to spirit
never ceases to hinder by age.
That whisper from my mother
carries birds from that of another.
Holding dear the original tongue
that spoke of truth, from brother to brother.
So, I lie upon her withering land, and
she shares secrets without reprimand.
A whisper so quiet the birds fall silent;
in the distance I hear a grain of sand.
To believe in your truth is obnoxious:
two faces crafted by redeeming conscience.
Searching for clues that prove integrity
is a wrongful doing by those who mock us.
Who are you to claim that spite and malice
shriek louder from hands so calloused?
When the whispers floating on the wind
say I'm worthy to drink from the chalice.

DECEPTIONS OF VIBRANCY

In a realm where shelves groan under
the weight of deceitful products,
the people's real essence is smothered
by corporate greed's stink.
Here, in this small store within a small, unsheltered town,
these items, they seem to think,
beckoning with their falsely vibrant hues.
Brought to life by unnatural forces that spawned them,
they murmur their synthetic falsehoods.
In my world, our status, our very value,
is gauged by our consumption.
Gradually, yet unyieldingly,
we morph into the very deceptions we crave.
Beneath my skin, within my bones,
a revolution stirs, pulsing with errors.
The floral lifeblood within me,
now replaced by binding waste.
Hypocrisy oozes from my lips
as I partake in the poisons
that dominate and subjugate
our once-pristine natural realm.

WHIRLWINDS OF WOMANHOOD

A restlessness breathes under my skin, which reminds me of the bloodshed from my mothers before. They encompass me with the howling winds of changing tides. We are the nurturers and builders of humanitarian structure. I wish to go back to a time when I believed that duplicity was plucking the flower from its roots whilst roaming upon the grass. The whirlwinds of calamity continue to transform the girl in me.

ABUSE OF POWER

Behind barriers lies a distorted story, uncontrolled.
Cruel hands to capture an intention to mold.
Push her face against the cold wall; she feels arduous.
An act that will appall, but no other could name dangerous.

In her solitude, she wrestles with her fears,
and beneath her skin, she hides with plastered ears.
But you, blinded by misguided morals that steer,
see her as a mere project—incomplete, unclear.

With words you pluck from your gray matter's root,
fill her mind with thoughts that send her mute.
Like a child's punishment, you chastise action;
yet unforgiving of the fact that you cause the reaction.

Manipulate her fragile mind of glass and
tell her she is unworthy, a smothered outcast.
But deep within, she begins to sense the shifting,
for she's more than lies, receptive and drifting.

She is human, seeking, searching for power.
Beyond your labels, she learns not to cower.
Hear her voice beyond silent screams spilling
from the depths of your lessons, unwilling.

TWENTY-THREE

In love's fling, I hear the intuitive third ring.
As they tell me opportune stories of the moon,
I sing to the power of three, and they echo my tune.

In two and three, born under the watch of duality,
I am balanced between two extremes and three dreams—
harmony with the risk of manifestation at the seams.

SILENT WITNESS

I speak on behalf of birthmarks,
veiled from the public's eye.
They are proof of the tragedies endured,
and the stability I could not defy.

OBSCURITY ISLAND

Off to the island! —she claims.
Where the world's lively obscurities
flourish in a land with no connection
to the tainted civilization of normality.

NEW PERCEPTION

The day after an agonizing day,
I searched for myself in my reflection,
and thought—
I am worthy of this chapter of my life.

HEALING SPELL

If I happen upon loneliness tonight,
show me healing in dreams of night.
May I cower in a wakeful rest;
perhaps I can befriend this guest.
I try to tame the wretched beast
hibernating for eternal feast.
As I sleep, so mote it be!
I ever mind my trust in thee.
Air above me, to hold my travel.
Earth below me, to bind the unravel.
Fire within me, to light the passion.
Water enclose me, to dampen the ashen.
Spirits surround me, fill this den:
I ask of thee, make me whole again.

LIVING IN FEAR

I dwell behind the murky walls within Dracula's castle.
Craving the light, I am left with the foul taste of decay.
My appetite for the wicked past shrieks at me,
like the bats who cast a shadow on my vision
with revelations of elsewhere.
I live my days in fear
of both the thing
that I've risen to be and you.
Perhaps there will be a day when I
will not be able to tell the difference.

CYCLES

We continue to meet
the past versions of us
who need saving.

THE STORY OF HANDS

Feel the rhythm of me tingling through my palms.
I search for you within the mazes built upon my fingertips.
The origins of me have no comparison to what comes yonder.
This is the story of hands that carry on the paramour's passion.
I miss the way your touch rose not only the bumps on my skin,
but the stars that shined on the fractures of my darkest secrets.
Hold me close to your heart and let me hold your hand in mine.
For your hands weave stories of their own with every sway.

DRUNK ON YOU

You are like the wine
that drips from my lips,
earthy and sweet. And as
I floated into drunkenness,
its perfume reminded me of
the complexities in your smile.

GROW WITH ME

Are you
growing or fluctuating,
showing or delegating,
because the end of our dreams
begin with these extremes—
and plateaus are so suffocating!

JAMAIS VU

The dual neurosis between us became unfamiliar,
but your lips were inviting and tasted of yesterday.

NEVER CEASE

She scrawled his name on the sliver of
paper ripped from a forgotten newspaper.
Even as the yellowed print wrinkled with dried
glass stains, his name thrived with eternal permanence.
One writer's infatuation soon becomes a man's immortality.

FIRE STARTER AND THE WOLF

He set her aflame for warmth she'd not share,
a love she withheld, coldly bare.
Yet she, like a wolf, hungered for his words so hollow,
devouring the emptiness, a sorrow to follow.
In their dance of ruin, they spun without tear;
a tragic duet—a rather toxic pair.

SISTER SUICIDE

She whispered the words that terrified my memories of her,
and I don't know if I lost air or gave it to her to hold close.

She spoke of dangerous nightmares and lonely desires,
and paralysis that came during the bumps in the night.

Sister Suicide had begged her for company that day,
and beyond her fears, she knew she had to be a big girl.

Thankful that I get to see her breath within this lifetime,
and I would not trade my memories for a polaroid of us.

ASK ME WHY

When we analyze behaviors
and unsee their intentions, we
fail to see the individual for
who they are—and that is a
misjudgment of one's
immediate character.

US FOUR

In shadows of a distant, faded home,
four siblings lived, yet lived alone.
Bound by blood, yet worlds apart,
each bore a deeply scarred heart.
The teddy bear, with a smile worn,
clutched in nights of silent scorn.
A comfort in the fleeting dark,
as soon as light, a mere remark.
In the corner, the outcast cast
perplexing questions no one asked.
Forgotten, shunned, a phantom pain,
in absent portraits, a hidden stain.
The nurturer, with an angry pace,
wore lines of grime upon her face.
The wisdom carried on her plate
was heavier than the mirror's weight.
The nomad, wild, never there—
because the floor was cold and bare.
A dirty stench and hair so matted,
girls so scared of men so tatted.

(continued)

(continued)

Mother locked in her bedroom lay,
drugs and toxins cover what may.
Yet time, a thief of anger's fire,
quenched the flames of dire mire.
The teddy bear, no longer just a toy,
and the outcast, heard with coy.
The nurturer, her strength radiates,
and the nomad, consistent in embrace.
Just like earth, water, fire, and air;
all so different, but always there.
My sisters are strong and pillars of wit.
Us four, from life—we take no fucking shit.

INFINITE SECOND

You know that it's love
when he challenges not
only your ambitions, but
the moments that lead to
an infinite second between.

SLEEP PARALYSIS

I woke up to him sitting slumped in front of me on the bed. His face peered down, covered by the blurred veil of a dreamy state. The surreal feeling left me unsettled as the cold seeped under my skin. Even the chill departed me after I saw the child on the ceiling. Its shaded shape crawled toward me with bent, man-like fingers. I was too terrified to scream, so I came to with a sense of dread and found that I was alone.

CHEMICAL CONFESSIONS

In a room where shadows hide and light is shy,
a child's eye, wide and wondering, silently pry.
Through a haze of confusion, her giver lies unclear,
engulfed in a ritual that ignites a long-term fear.
Her heart, a tiny drum, beats with unspoken questions,
as she watches a parent, lost in chemical confessions.
The air is thick with a secret, one the girl could never find,
leaving trails of worry in a young and innocent mind.
Whispers of neglect reach out to the girl for a hug,
in darkness, she watches her parent pick up the drug.
Eyes that once sparkled with stories and laughter,
now swim in a sea of what may come after.
In her small hands, toys are forgotten,
as she witnesses a love, fractured and rotten.
The innocence of youth, tangled in an adult's strife,
a child caught in the crossfire of another's life.

ESCAPING LOVE

A mourning on the morning of...
I watched as the cars drove past;
pondering, while the trees cast
a shadow on the cage of love.

GASLIT

Day or night, which is it, I ponder?
Right or wrong, in this blur, I wander.
Reality twists in your uncertain light,
warping my world, blurring my sight.
Your words, like live wires, shock and confine,
zapping truth, weaving lies into a vine.
In this tangle, my path fades to grey,
yet audaciously, you urge me to stay.
Through the veil of lies, my eyes finally see,
distorting my intentions, but I break free.
In the clarity of truth, I've come to find,
the lessons you cast, now clear in my mind.

POINT-BLANK

Point your woven finger at me again,
and see what happens to my eyes.
I am perplexed by the sounds of you—
hurt by your condemning disguise.
You say I do the very thing I do not;
fastening my integrity like a name tag.
I search within for the courage to be real.
Your face is red and warm while you brag.
I thought that I helped pull the trigger
that caused us both to tumble down.
All you did was fire the gun; point-blank,
and left me alone in this wretched hometown.

OPPORTUNITY COST

I thought it was efficiency motivating me to streamline you, but laborious it was to try to improve you without the risk analysis. I understand the complexities that get lost in transformation; however, your transactional approach geared toward control. I thought that there would be a loss to the potential of losing you, but without input, one cannot make a marginal difference—and I'm tired of the costs always outweighing the benefits of affection.

PLEASE

I need you.
Is that what you want to hear?
I am dependent on you.
Perhaps that is what you fear?
I cannot love with balance, it seems.
Either too little or too much,
and I rip apart at the seams;
trying to justify my love for someone
who only loves me in their dreams.

SEIZE PERMISSION

Let us be spontaneous
and meticulous in our
quest for pipe dreams.

KARMIC CHAOS

You are in love with your own chaos.
And you've been taught to love obsessively,
dependent on the oddities that breath deep within you.
Equal parts clever and critical and calm.
Between the karmic couple came
the calculated and the hectic.
Here you stand; finally
honoring all of you.

TO THE FRIENDS WHO KNEW ME WELL

I think about you often, because you still carry a version of me that only lives in the shadows of my mind. These recollections that play like a record remind me of your eyes, and I fear that the distance between us roams back and forth like the phantoms that haunt my silent apartment. I miss you, but I'm afraid to reach out. I hear your laughter calling me back towards another distant memory.

ABANDONING SELF

I was overwhelmed by my own complexities,
and it was easier to run away from myself
than it was to search through the ghost towns within.

CONGRUENCY

In domains of congruent angles, tangled.
a square is a rectangle but not in reverse.
I think about this often in terms of my comforts.
Happiness always leads to the gain of serenity;
however, our comfortabilities do not always
lead us to peace of mind. Beliefs wander, pondering
my potential for happiness extending beyond
the parameters I place around my comforts.

PARANOID PAST

The pressure is suppressed for now—but it lingers like the thoughts of uncertainty, obsessively and inarticulately nagging on the child in me.

My mind restlessly focuses on the peripherals of my envisioned past, and I am paranoid of the person I have chosen to be just to survive.

INWARD

I glanced toward the window and the
condensation painted dull hues on the glass.

I dreaded the idea that the new year would
appear as empty as this rendered window.

I considered the irony behind my lack of
sight beyond this monotonous display.

I am remembering to search inward for self
in this approach toward accomplishment.

HAIKYOU

I ache for your touch.
Detrimental remedy.
I fear the unknown.

PROTECTIVE PARALLELS

With a collective typeface, we're letters in the same design,
distinct in intention, yet alike in the rhythm of our minds.
My fascination with your intellect, a parallel to my fear—
of drawing near, yet holding back, in uncertainty's revere.

You stirred currents of my thoughts, a muse in protective grace,
with an avid quest for growth, in every dream and space.
Yet, in the sway of closeness, I retreated from your flame,
A tender man who knew my essence, not just my middle name.

PURPLE SKIES

Fabricate me stories of a
world with purple skies,
but please don't build a dream
in me and tell me lovely lies.

ROMANTICIZING

I grew up fantasizing about romance being a conditioned union with perfect-timings, love letters, and comfortability. And when I stepped out into the world, I found that the censored truth was but only a fragment of the conflicts I'd experience. Love is not lust, nor is it the lack thereof. Love does not answer the underlying question, "Do you complete me in spirit and in matter?" The concept of romance manifests a solidity in a dependent form of passion. Love does not offer the heart in hopes that the other offers theirs, but rather extends a hand to hold when the weight of existence is too heavy to bear. I learned that nobody could complete half of me, otherwise I cannot have the capacity to be my fullest self. I continue to suppose that romance is a sentimental sacrifice of character; however, in truth, love is a means to a beginning. It is both a mindset and an action, but also an emotion and a stillness. The theories and practicalities of love contradict the innate independence we crave. Despite fundamental differences that coexist amongst lovers, there is a collective value in the depths of assembly. The girl in me is aware of the trepidation that grows in the presence of such infatuation. Nevertheless, to love in this world is to both sacrifice self and build upon another.

STEADFAST PILLAR

Vow to listen to the silence where my words cease to tread;
to decipher the sharp gazes where my eyes are often led.

Vow to sense the lingering warmth when from your side I stray;
to know my ties to you remain steadfast, come what may.

Vow to perceive the light in me, even when I am blind;
to see that I am venturing far from the life I've left behind.

Vow to cherish me as I learn to embrace my own soul;
to be my steadfast pillar, as I journey toward being whole.

DEMONS

Hit me again.

Afterall, that is how your words feel when
you let your demons out of their cage.

WEEP FOR THE WEAK

If tears are for the weakest, as some claim,
why then at birth, our very first refrain
is crying loud, as we're swept into light,
a natural call on earth's very first sight?

ABYSMAL

Ode to abyss,
I search through
clear nothings to
find only a fragment
of who you used to be.

WRITER'S REQUIEM

Do I self-sabotage
to escape writers block?

As I plagued my journal
with secrets and requiems,
the veil lifted, uncovering
the real reason why I could
not let go of the shame within.

COULDA WOULDA SHOULDA

I could rest and tally my tears,
but that would never cease my fears.
Perhaps I should reach out to peers,
but could that lead to judging ears?
I dread that I would grind their gears;
perchance I should peruse my years,
then I could learn from which adheres:
nothing would be as it appears!
Till then I should search vast frontiers.

CLATTER AND GOLD

I am not the things you say.
Pieces clatter in disarray,
yet I am dipped in gold.
Placed upon a pedestal;
clothed little animal,
yet I am trapped within.
You find beauty in my chaos.
I search for solitary séance,
yet find no reason to be loved.
You think of me a goddess,
but these demons—they haunt us,
yet you keep me in your arms.

COPING

I drew upon my wrists
little black stars in order
to distract myself from
the pain of losing you.

Because I already knew
that drawing blood was
only going to cause me
grief in losing myself.

INTOXICATE ME

I don’t know which to get
intoxicated from tonight:
this cheap bottle of vodka,
or your words I reread in my mind.
Both cause me to stumble over the
perception I have of myself.

AUTHENTICATION

Digital people copy and paste,
but I still edit myself with fleeting dreams,
processed caffeine, and the urges to be someone I'm not.

THE OVERTHINK

Be wary of the thoughts of the Overthink,
for they place commentary on my memories.
Thought after so, I question my truth as I drink
from which this place creeps. I surely shrink
into intrinsic outbursts that blur boundaries.

I am a yes-girl here, my habits hold shame.
The Overthink lays a compelling trance,
and I am stripped like a face with no name.
Tragic as a moth determined toward flame,
this manifestation is home by happenstance.

ENMESHING

I whistled in the lone darkness,
trudging my way through my past doubts.
And slow I went nevertheless,
as if I could just evanesce:
who knows about my whereabouts?
Call me complex or call my phone,
you will receive the same answer.
For who am I to cast a stone
upon the girl I used to know;
she dances but is no dancer.
I am troubled by my defeat
that I create in my own mind.
Solace is a friend I must meet.
Blurred by the enmesh, bittersweet.
My sacrifice has been assigned.

WORDS WRUNG

My versions of them murmur to me
from the slanted realms within;
lucidly and captivating.

I hear mumblings from my fingertips,
and they guide me to tell their stories—
listen! A witness of words wrung.
I am all parts them, and they are born
from sticky note translations, scrawled,
and raised under ink pens and rows of keys.

UNSPOKEN PARANOIA

I am not alone.
They live in the walls like the thoughts
that hide away in my mind, unclean.
Find them, for I seek words no more
than the freedom to use them, unseen.
Ahem! Get the fuck out of my head,
onto sheets of paper, ream after ream.
Defeated, my purpose hides like my
reality lost in a day dream.

WISE OR FOOLISH

In pursuit of wisdom's irrationality, I yearn—
for where else must we dwell to learn?
To grow with a burning passion
requires an absurdity in turn.

FOSTER KID

I am in search of her in between the spaces
of the letters I read in novels, wordless.
Escaping amongst drawings from years of
line sketch and deformed ink portraits,
she roams here and there between the doorway
dividing the loose and the scripted;
not as a ghost dragging along a pale lantern,
but as a wolf in the land of the cryptic.
Rummaging through photos that did not make
the cut into an estate sale of my crumbs,
she sits patiently in purple, hands crossed,
juxtaposed to the woman that I have become.
Although I swim through towering waves of
memory to kiss the scars on the child in me,
I find that she is present in all versions of myself,
from the healed to the fragmented debris.

PALPITATE

I don't want to write statements and call it poetry.
I want to bleed connotation throughout the veins
that wrap my body. I want to feel a moments
palpitation reverberate upon the walls of the
atriums in my chest. Give me heartache,
—and I'll give you words.

ENFOLDING THOUGHTS

I lose you but come to
and find that that is life
as we appreciate it to be.
Alas, I always find you
within restless thoughts
and unspoken enfoldings.

LIES WITHIN MY BONES

Shards of hollow words pierce
the blue tongue until swollen
cheeks suffocate validity that
lies within my bones.
It is but a persistent ache
in which fashions a sting
that seems to animate
lies within my bones.
Catch a gander at the cherry
face with roaming eyes of
meek insecurity which
lies within my bones.
Rough simplicity forms words
from an imitated smile where
a new profound freedom now
lies within my bones.

GOLDEN

The shame you place on me weighs me down
harder than the gravity that pulls at my knees.
It is all but a whisper—silent enough to slide
through thoughts but loud enough to burst the
knots that are loosely bound around my image.
Your comparisons are sharp, and slithers toward
me as uncertainty peels from my bones, like a
second pair of skin. I hear a violin performing
the lullabies that used to chase away monsters
hiding behind my reflection. I am an extension
of a beaten statistic. And beaten, I am, in a race
between me, her, and the others who face guilt.
Built into a pleaser, I plead— "please save her!"
Left in golden light, this inexactness blinds me.
What is my ambiance? For lustrous yellow does
not match the blue hues under my skin. I begin
to shield myself from traumas bleeding within.

OUR THING

I will see you in the dreams we dream.
I will always be waiting there for you.

PERFUME

If I could capture your scent
and transfer it into a bottle,
I would hide it underneath my
pillow because I would be to
troubled in running out of you.

INSOMNIA

The knots in the wood crawled across the desk before me, as I stared with sleep-deprived eyes. The dim light shone on the backs of hungry flies disguising themselves as parts of the furniture. And I could not tell if I was awake or dreaming; for there was no distinction between the buzzing of the flies and the ringing in my ears. Perhaps the pronunciation was the same.

I felt insentient, yet wide-awake as my world around me took its breath. Hazy doppelgangers of heinous light danced upon the hairs on my skin, and vertigo swept me up like the sprites calling me towards their dreams. It had been a lunar passing since they had last seen me, so I closed my eyes and allowed consciousness to dissolve into a lesser version of me.

BACKWASH

Here lies the backwash of a poem,
tossed back into a sea of letters that make
up words hidden behind fastened lips.
A wave of the tongue and I am flooded
by the tears of those who do not know me,
canceled; lost within the bubbles claimed.
I hear my voice, but I am no siren, as the
salt seeps into the pores of my skin. I am
wrinkled, like my conventional certainties.
Take your backwash—it is not mine to drink,
for we all travel from foreign land of preference
and I will carry my cargo without your pressing spit.

TRANSITIONING THOUGHTS

Be clear with the meanings and pulsings of your deliberations. You are disassociated between him and the you that you identify. Listen to the way his tone holds bold attitude, no concealing there. His silence demands attention, but you take time with your reflections. You question your own intentions and are comforted by the white noise. Her purring rhymes with your heartbeat, as you engage transitioning thoughts.

DARKNESS DIES

Look up at your god
in the somber skies and
realize that he sits upon
white-washed clouds.
Close your eyes, the
darkness dies as you
watch the light waltz
upon your lids; painting
films of who you could be.
But the world lies.

ANXIETY ATTACK

I disappear through words printed
on creased sheets, screaming:
Let go of me! I have things to do—
They breath down my neck, and
I am frozen in a state of intangibilities.
They hold me; intrusive to my space,
and I cannot place a grasp on my palm.
Watch me through the glass, perching
on a sill of weeds bent from midwinter.
I implode in my abode, density rises, and
I ask myself the question: why is the matter
that squeezes my chest so collapsing here?

DAY ONE

One day,
I will dissolve
invasive tones
that fester lies
that weigh a ton.

One day,
I will value my
potentials that
are engrained
in me, finespun.

One day,
I will express my
amity with myself
when I say that
today is day one.

PATH TO FORGIVENESS

Tangled crossroads tremble underneath boots,
broken-in from playgrounds and slippery slopes.
My demons used to keep me company on this path;
but after forgiving the parts of me that carry criticism,
they have left me to tread alone under the shade of serenity.

PLATEAU

Dearest me from ages preceding,
You will lose control over the idea
that your worth is leaning porous.
You may question trifling things,
like what to wear on your flesh.
And astronomical things, such as
what to wear on your shirt sleeve.
Your cheeks will burn when you
trial a lie, and fluttering moths will
become a warning sign for change.
You'll notice a peripheral proclivity
for creatives around you; however,
these ventures may pull a quick one
before the moon has a chance to rest.
Days will pass into the next, and you
will become an intimidation to that
girl traveling through the vineyards.
Do not believe the skeptics when they
claim that reality cannot be a fantasy,
for my eyes create my own perception.
That is not to say that truth is malleable.
Although tragedy is no exception to the
woman you will become, hear me when
I tell you that a plateau is only a mindset.

COMPOSURE

Equanimity is a collected rumor
that rarely reaches the ears of the
oil-burners and the depraved creatives.
We were not taught through composure,
but through the tingling of our nerves.

CATASTROPHICALLY DIFFERENT

We both were obsessed with catastrophe.
The difference between you and I was that you embraced
the calamities of suffering, and I ruminated in the adoration.

BLESSED BE

Serenity for me is imagining myself
screaming into the boundless oblivion of the ocean,
and summoning the goddesses on the
horizon line to scream back.

SUMMARIZING LIFE BEYOND ADDITION

I am not the sum of my parts,
but the multiplication of words
formed through fits and starts.

WATCHING ME

Always observing me—this abyss
has a million eyes to trace my space
and a trillion mouths that don't dismiss.

DISARRAY

I dove into myself to write this
collection of reflections and discovered
that these words will never end.
I am beyond characters that make up
words that make up lines that make
up verses that make up poems that
make up stories that make up pieces of me.
Free is who I get to be when I create.
I am this body as this vessel is my craft
words toss in like waves,
shaking symbols in the raft.
And I am aroused by the idea that
someday and somehow in some way
I just may fall in love with someone
who talks a bit of disarray.
Because, I am one who is moved by words:
a qualifier to a life of sacrifice.
Suffering, creation and dandelions are three of the same—
each slowly breaking down what's underneath the surface.
All word-collectors love the burn of enduring flame.
Acquire me a man who thinks he is the one to blame,
perhaps then I find a likewise mind
who may offer his last name.

BE THAT CLICHÉ

The misconception with clichés in contemporary society is not that they lack original thought, but the stigma behind their overuse contributes to the idea that we all label what's around us. Many believe that labels create chaotic curves toward guilty verdicts; however, they assist with humanistic organization and the simplification of interpretation. The truth is that we all crave to be heard as we all connect to each other's metaphors. We all throw around ordinariness and stereotypes, but to apply our own experiences is to be original in context. The real concern is not the cliché, but the assumption that what is being said is not authentically expressed. Intention is half the drive, and despite the incomplete excess of stereotypes and clichés, there is a lesson present upon originality that must be situationally observed.

THE FAWNING

Holding onto something real,
the memories become a shield.
She lifts her blade slow and strong.
The fawning is over; the battle is on.

UNBIND

I can hear the fire taunting me, cackling
as it spreads over my roots, crackling—
I am bound to archaic fate that whispers over the sea.
The undertones of my ancestors tell me that I am free.
Give me power to see those trying to force subjugation.
Uncover the truth that rests stagnant under my foundation.
To unveil is to unbind—how many times must I remind you
that I have already paid off debts that you claim are overdue.
I beg to breathe, but how many scores must I afford.
You expose your teeth, and I unsheathe my sword.
Fight for fight, my right is engraved in stone,
and you have the audacity to insult me upon the throne.
Do not pull me to your level, and then call me a stranger.
This is my life I am building, and I am proud of these changes.

NON-APOLOGY

You say you will never see me as your equal,
but I am finding sympathy in this.
For, who am I to be in charge of emotions
that aren't mine, if you do not care for how
I feel in the crashing of reliant tides?
We can be congruent without pointing fingers or telling lies.
I will not take responsibility for your feelings
after my response to your derogatory alibis.

MOTHER'S HYMN

Hold me, for a mother's love binds trust.
Mold me from pieces
that fall from your star dust.

I'm yearning for your encouraging tone,
burning a passion for
the loyalties in stone.

Mind me, as I look to you for womanhood.
Remind me that I'm standing in
the prints where you've stood.

From which lessons of love, affection, and identity come,
the retrieval of feminine
worth grows and hums.

REMOVING DYSFUNCTION

Love is more than sex, and a relationship is more than love.
Respect me as I find the words to express myself thereof.
I repress the logical part of me for the sake of being with you.
And, over time I have treated myself as I have been raised to do.
You do the same things on the daily;
your dysfunction teaches me
that my worth is more developed than your immaturity.
I must break this cycle of appeal
toward deprived and eerie persons.
For my ambitions are ample, and with you, my dreams worsen.
Let me find a simpler way across this empty plain.
Each time I break it off, toward myself I release my disdain.
Help me please, anybody—they always pull me out.
But, again, I lean on needy people, because alone,
I'm afraid of my own doubt.

DUST REVEALS

You emotionally ignore me,
immaturity seeps on through.
Listen to the words you say,
I'm yearning for a corkscrew.
I give you what you desire, and
you want me for my body.
I always ponder your intentions:
what would you do with a carbon copy?
While you sleep or play the day away,
I'm inching closer to my ideals.
That requires a detachment,
and the dust between us reveals.

TURNING THE PAGE

Do I look familiar?
Something about this
is novel—peculiar.
I feel grounded in me,
dancing to this decree:
I learn by the power of three,
and I am no longer an intruder.

ANTI-POEM

I
will
not
follow
the
line
to
chow hall
and call
my
verses
that
in
which
is
not
poetry.

COUNT AND ERASE

My hunger gnaws, yet thoughts of nourishment consume me.
Indulgence feels like a breach of self-set rules, like impropriety.
Instead, I choose restraint, lean on mere supplements for aid.
Down I spiral into deceit, my raccoon eyes in darkened shade.
As my waist contracts, so does my demeanor, tightly wound.
I ponder the natural rhythms that once my body soundly found.
Yet now, my self-view fades, a shadow, lost and out of place.
Like the calories I count and erase, my words too leave no trace.

EVALUATE YOUR STANDARDS

When I excused their ways, their toxicity found room to stay,
an open door for harmful cycles, repeating day after day.
I learned in delay, that beneficial doubts cost me years.
While freely given, like flyers to pity parties, drawing near.

To men immature, seeking kindness without a price to pay,
my compassion's fee, towering like debts they never sway.
Requests I made, liabilities to some, within view,
as I questioned my standards, whether fair or askew.

Was it wrong to seek less than perfection's highest tier?
The fault I found, not in hopes, but ambitions I hold here.
Those lacking depth in passion, or a thirst to truly see,
must be struck off the list from prospects, best fucking agree.

For only those who value complexity, and see me as I am,
deserve a place within my world, part of my life's long plan.

EPILOGUE

The day before my last page of this chapter,
I thought about the epilogue wanting to begin.
Herein, will be the reflections of a girl with no skin.

I thought that ghostwriting was a form of expression,
and although staying reserved was enlightening,
stagnation stings, and it was all on a budget of shoestring.

Exposing the truth is difficult when you lie to yourself,
as the sake of others paints portraits of doppelganger images.
Cursed lineage! Oh—the message I was looking for
took damage.

If your lover was a friend before benefits, it wouldn't feel
like friends with benefits—both of us spoke riddles and rhyme,
a dime is what I'd give to see your growth after this last time.

This is different in all ways, yet intrinsically aligned.
Don't lie to yourself for the advantage of others;
a veil covers our sacrifice. I turn the page, and fear smothers.

REMINDED

If there is anything that I am not,
frivolous comes to mind.
But when I linger in the afterthought,
I am reminded of the worth you viewed in me, blind.

VIRTUAL UNSTRING

Learn about me through the capacities between us,
rather than through virtual unstring.
You think I'm leaving you with the dust that flies behind me,
but the things you say to me happen to sting.
Don’t gaslight me and say that I like everyone but you
when you are the one who chooses to think that way.
Hear my words without digital literacies, and you just may
find that your commentary is the reason I choose not to stay.

ODYSSEY

In this new journey, my aim isn't to stand apart from others, but to evolve beyond the girl I once was: timid, easily swayed. Walking in my own shoes, unique paths unfold, not meant for comparison. Advice flows freely, as does the shadow of depression gnawing at my worth. Yet, I realize the truest guidance comes from within—from the woman I am becoming, brimming with potential.

DELUSION

I continued to lie to myself,
because I didn't like the person I had become.
This bled into my anxiety for how they saw me,
and I continued to lie to the ones I loved.

LEAVE ME SPEECHLESS

Vulnerability is my favorite type of cringe.
There is a level of unease within the exposed
capacities between us, but I think this tension is
equal parts awkward and compelling.

I am selling the idea that you and I deserve
such openness to hold space for the complexities
that breath in us, and I can feel from you a sense of
chaotic energy that reminds me of my roots.

What constitutes this underlying awareness?
You are not demanding in movement, and I appreciate the
reassurance you give through the natural fluctuation
of your energy—you leave me speechless.

UNDER THE SKIN

Words and stones
may scratch her bones,
but time will never heal.
Cut her once,
her skin will close
but the dignity was easy to steal.
Cut her twice,
she learns to sacrifice
her skin to speak the truth.
Cut her once more,
from skin and worth easily torn,
the bone is exposed and wounded.
Growing and running
while her oppressor is grinning,
she despises the woman she has become.
Although her skin
heals over scrapes hiding within;
she is learning trust, but the pain resides herein.

ENTANGLED

When love finds its way, how shall I then know?
In quiet replies to quirks that you show.
In wisdom found in words, in acts so kind;
and past flaws shared, like old tales intertwined.

Your dreams laid out, like breadcrumbs in tow,
reveal a world unseen, where mysteries may grow.
The curve of my smile, in your thought, I find,
a moment's pause, as two hearts seek to be aligned.

Sweet as honey on nights, embraced by a protector,
far from the loneliness where sorrows could fester.
But how to recognize a love as deep as this?
Can it be known why I've fallen hard for his kiss?

In your grasp, it feels right to hope for our series.
I have trust in you, so hold me—let's entangle our stories.

TOO COMPLEX

In depths of who I am, a maze reveals;
where complexities breed, and complexities heal.
Like their opinions, my thoughts intertwine.
My goddesses hear me, intricately divine.

Oh—how I thirst for a simpler way,
but my complexities thrive, and they never stray.
Dancing and twirling, they never relent,
providing me with a unique temperament.

I am a world of contradictions, it seems.
A labyrinth full of paradoxes and themes.
My mind is a battleground of beliefs and ideals,
where complexities flourish and feelings appeal.

At times, I may overthink, lost in my haze.
I create complexes and a perplexing daze.
But within this chaos lies a glory I must share.
The depths of me claim water, fire, earth, and air.

For it is through my complexities, I find,
a remarkable image, sharp and refined.
In the intricacies lies my power, foreseeing.
A reflection of the deepness within my being.

IN THE COSMOS

In the sky there’s a tale rather untold,
of a love that's ancient, with a story so old.
The moon and the sun, a flawless pair,
bound by destiny, light and air.
The sun, with his intense golden hue,
radiates warmth; his brilliance is true.
Perhaps a warning of promise and shine,
drunk on his radiance and dandelion wine.
But in the darkness, ethereal stars do appear,
and there, a cosmic beauty comes near.
The moon, with her shimmering glow,
casts a calm silver stillness below.
As daylight fades and the night takes hold,
the sun descends, his rays controlled.
The moon ascends, her face luminous,
two celestial beings, time is voluminous.
In their galactic dance, they ebb and flow,
embracing each other, a tangled beau.

(continued)

(continued)

The sun, with passion, caresses the moon,
while the moon, with grace, reflects his tune.
Their love, an ever-eternal embrace,
a harmony found in age and in space.
For when the sun needs solace to find,
the moon holds him gently, never unkind.
And when the moon yearns for a gentle remedy,
the sun's rays reach out, unafraid of complexity.
So, let us learn from this solar scene,
that true love thrives through constant routine.
For even when nothingness tries to smother,
the sun and moon will always hold each other.

OBLIVION

They burrow.
The white space expands across this wretched page.
Oblivion. Why:
Must my hands wrinkle to the sound of your absence?
You were supposed to be there.
I cannot tear this unbearable page. Aging
in words that burrow under white silence and sage.

CHANGE MY MIND

They propose their approach, outlined.
How do I tell them that I change my mind?
I want to explore decisions without burden;
to embrace myself when I feel uncertain.

Their words may drift in the seas of persuasion,
but my heart, mind, and body crave its destination.
This journey is a novel that I'll read, if I dare.
I'm learning autonomy, so they best beware.

Respecting their wisdom, I lend an ear.
I absorb the narratives that they hold dear.
Yet, within is a message that I cannot dispose;
it's whispering secrets that I plan to disclose.

I think about the choices I made long ago:
can I echo their approach and still happen to grow?
Well, I gather my courage and I speak my truth.
Without fearing their judgment, I follow my roots.

For change is the principle of being alive,
it's the glimmer that assists our spirits to thrive.
Though they may shake their heads in dissent,
I won't be swayed by their words of intent.

(continued)

(continued)

I stand tall with the strength of my being,
ready to embrace the unknown; foreknowing.
It’s never too late to turn things around.
I think it’s okay to let your guard down.

So, let me wander through uncharted terrain,
where a hawthorn tree grows without disdain.
With each step, I declare my independence;
embracing that of which I’ll give to my descendants.

No longer afraid to stray away from all I’ve known,
I stitch my own path that is perfectly sewn.
For in these footsteps, I build upon my power;
I have witnessed a shift that will not let me cower.

So, let them tell me to echo their approach.
I want them to suppose that I’m beyond reproach.
With the courage to stand firm; I am now aligned.
I'll tell them proudly, "I've changed my mind."

THE PLETHORA

I ghostwrite their experiences,
and nobody knows.
Feel their pain, let it rain,
and we privately rest juxtaposed.
I see them through a local reality
as I am touched by their aura.
Composing drafts from
intuitive analysis,
I am aware of the plethora.
There are no ordinary limitations
that pull me away from this.
I practice my grounding,
the bonds are bounding,
and I am left to reminisce.

BIDDING FAREWELL

I hear your phantom calls
echoing in my mind,
as my purity screams,
I am lost in a bind.
Down these halls of the
memories, fading and thin.
I weave them from threads
spinning within.
In the shadows, I stumbled
upon your wretched ghost,
a mysterious presence
of melancholy, engrossed.
Your whispers are haunting
like a distant call,
toward a reminder of love,
lost in the fall.
But my purity—oh,
how it screams to be free!
Locked away,
longing for its jubilant flee.
It echoes through the corridors,
where love once gleamed
in faded remnants of a dream.

(continued)

(continued)

I trace these dark and hallowed halls,
where your voice resonates,
my purity brawls.
With memories that you
thought were swell,
leaving traces of sorrow,
as they bid farewell.
Yet, in this somber dance
of recollections and pain,
I find solace in the notes
of a tougher refrain.
Though your calls linger like
whispers on the breeze,
I'll find strength for
my soul to appease.
And with each line drawn,
my purity shall bloom,
a masterpiece of words,
dispelling all gloom.
I'll listen to your phantom calls,
as they slowly diminish,
embracing my love,
unmarked by this blemish.

POPPIN'

She said my poetry
is like Mary Poppins,
none of it makes any sense.
But she will surely learn
the lessons life presents.

Passionate and clever,
that girl is like a racehorse.
She takes her challenges
like spoonfulls of sugar
that commences the course.

Brilliant and beautiful,
that girl is practically perfect
in all the ways; admiring.
I hope she keeps that spark in her heel,
and that wonder in her eye; inspiring.

DROWN OR BREAK

In depths so deep,
I find myself drowning.
Voices are screaming,
within arms' reach sounding:
"You ought to swim," they claim,
with defeated eyes upon me,
they stare at my face.
Suffocated and trapped,
my cries to the surface are replaced
with rapids of silent echoes within.

And amidst the pressure,
I must seek my own voice.
Within darkness that dwells,
I can still have a choice for
who will I be if I cannot be free?
Must I wrinkle to words
that they throw at me.

With each gasp for air,
I question my privilege.
Blame me, but they pushed
me right over that edge.

(continued)

(continued)

My lungs ache for the sweetest inhale,
and I think that I've found that,
but how do I know when to sail?

So many questions,
I feel so confined
in this stifling stage,
binding body and mind.
I am soaked in this pain,
but this is my time to decide:

should I continue to drown
or break through this tide?

FABLES

I am learning to stand my ground.
You try to silence me with a dark voice, renowned.

Invalidate me, belittle my past.
You say that your hardships are greater, surpassed.

My childhood traumas, I carry them in
my failures and passions and successes, herein.

Do not damage my stories, they are not fables.
They matter to me, and I am finished with your labels.

STRESSOR

Stress, you see, is holding me confined.
These courses are bitterly refined.
Help me find the path of knowledge,
where I will not be defined.
I seek to advance the pieces of my mind.

Despite the pressure I feel, I won't succumb.
How can you learn through habits that numb?
These lessons are challenging, but I overcome,
because healthy stress allows me to become someone.

TRUSTING

Searching for the remnants displaced;
I cannot forget the look on your face.
Tell me to reason, pick fun at my cry.
How could you honestly tell me to die?
I believed in you and your words sunk through;
all of the people I love suffered too.
Do not look at me with love in your eyes,
I turn my back, and then you whisper lies.
There is a portion of me that I dedicate to you,
this familiarity is difficult for me to construe.

MEANT TO BE

I glance back,
a tender touch I see.
A gentle masculinity
staring back at me.
Whisper words uncanny,
while your lips rest on my
neck. Mysterious and true,
I fear you see me as a shipwreck.
It's okay to feel far away from
the things you've lost at sea.
We'll find that gentle touch again,
where we are meant to be.

BE YOUR OWN

This world will try to preach
a truth that disregards your reach.
My sweet—you were taught to conceal,
and believe that love for you isn't real.
It is time for a secret, that you may find:
be willing to show that life can be kind.
You have a right to choose who you want to be.
You can be your own, that is my guarantee.

INFATUATED

He likes me in green,
it brings out my eyes.
The minutes collide;
a timeless revise.
He's high on my smile;
I feel translated.
We're one of the same,
infatuated.

TRANSPIRING

Let us turn the page and end the chapter
that rained on us from prior.
The gleam I feel when I am with you
is a feeling I admire.
Be my world and I will be your sunshine,
and this love will spread like wildfire.
Brighten me with your gaze;
for these timeless moments arouse the gods,
and they want us to transpire.

THE UNRAVELING

I am taking accountability in all areas of my life. That includes my past mistakes. That includes my successes. My identity derives from a place that is centered within myself, and the guilt in me dissipates as I remember all those moments when you claimed to be true to me. Are you afraid of who I have turned out to be? Were you dreading this moment where I would stand up and proclaim that my life is my own? You came into my life when I was still trying to learn how to approach the world while the traumas were still fresh in memory. And as I feel this string unravel, I murmur to my goddess the secrets I've learned about me. I will leave all of you who claim that my individuality is a trophy won through control. This is the unraveling of a woman who no longer gives a damn for the men who has turned her emotions against her.

SETTLING FOR MORE

You think you know what's best for me, but you struggle with what's best for you. I am living and learning and growing, and that takes experience. I don't want to have these expectations of self to hold me back from the potential of love—so, I'm going to give it a try. I want to settle, and it's okay to want that. I grew up with the words "don't settle for anything less than what you deserve" ingrained in the ridges of my mind. I did not feel good enough, so I learned how to run away instead. However now, to settle is to *decide*. It's to feel secure in a new situation. Settling does not have to mean that I am paying a debt or silencing myself. I have enough experience to understand the balance between extremes, and I cannot practice that balance if I don't attempt comfortable consistency. I can still be ten steps ahead, but I'm tired of expecting the worst in everyone that enters my life. I have learned what love is not, and I have learned how to approach my anxieties healthily. I'm an adult now, and I can't continue to jump around from one decision to the next like an impatient wanderer lost in herself. I deserve better, yes—we all do. But there is a difference between my life and yours. Let me feel what I am supposed to. I know you have good intentions but do not psychoanalyze me. Not every person out there is a threat. If you think I carry myself so well, and that I should continue having high expectations, then why are you questioning my choices? Afterall, I wouldn't be doing as well without my own preferences. Therefore, hear me. I know you might think I'm settling, but that is your opinion. I have learned the value of making my own judgments and settlements.

EXTREMES

Get a grip, girl.
Sailing,
yet I can't decree
which extreme
I should live today.
This disarray
leads me to
thoughts of you,
and I seem to want
to stay.

DAWNING

Memories of you
that scream at me
tune with the distant
sounds of dogs barking—
sparking darkening pools
in your eyes; I'm deceived by
dawning dreams of your disguise.

FREE TO BE

I want to get out of my head—
feel fully invigorated by the
potentiality of experience.
I have trained my whole childhood
to be the beholder of my daydreams.
Transformed, the girl in me screams.
The winds of change toss me to and fro,
the birds know, and it blooms into spring.

I am free to be, she said, just me.
No apologies—and I believed her.
This reminds me to read the fine print
on the drawers within my subconscious.
Those memories are explored, and adding
more experiences as I process the last leads
me to question the validity of my anxieties.

PREMONITION

Tell me what I don't want to hear,
because at the end of the day,
I'll be pleased knowing that
someone out there sees what I see.
To be faced with the truth
can be alarming in denial;
premonition is the forerunner
to a life without contradiction.
So, tell me how the words sound
that dribble from my movements;
they rhyme with the words
inside my mind.

SHAPE

People claim it's not the froth
that gathers at their sides.
Indeed, they feel there's no bond
between their soul and hides.

But I hold the belief that I encompass
everything within and around,
for isn't it true that my attitudes
shape my physical ground.
This existence we forge is
undeniably profound.

RIVER OF WISHES

Wishes floated past, one by one, as he held me close. He shivered with the fish at our ankles, as we cast the rod in release. The trees quivered and created shadows around the perimeter, despite the real mystery behind his lips. The dragonfly, dark and blue, rested with us and every time it flew away, it happened to find its comforts back within our company. A blue heron soared by, singing about opportunity that resides in stillness. This river, this romance, this man, this memory—the wait was worth it.

VALI-DATE WITH SELF

Lost in the archives of
those who understood me;
words drenched,
ink ran down the walls in my mind.
The pages wrinkled
like the skin around my eyes
after crying over years of
experiences that stood mistaken.
I will read these words again,
and again, and again—and
this crowded collection of
recollections leaves me satisfied
in the idea that the only person
who can make changes in
my life is me.

SECOND THOUGHTS

He thought he was too much,
and I thought I was too little.
He thought in waves of second-guessings,
and I thought my words were brittle.

QUIET FLIRTATION

You know that I have words
hidden under my skin.
You leave the air astonished,
and I take stage of such unravels.
Let's assume desperation is a mockery
for those who cannot find infatuation.
You continue to love me
for the words I cannot say;
our quiet flirtation.

REPEATING

I am stuck replaying my validations,
as chaotic rhymes fill the damp air.
My wet hair after that shower presses me.
Impressed with my reflection, I stand.

Crowded by thoughts that tick, tick, tick;
like clockwork, and it makes me sick.

Why does the blackbird with yellow eyes
sit still on my sill? I cannot despise
these questions of mine that pull me closer to the
thought that I love myself more than you do.
love myself.
love myself.
love myself.
love myself.
love myself more than I have ever had.

HEATHER

The heather that grows around my heart
bleeds when I think of you, and I come to.
There are pages torn at the corners, but
I am proud to say that I was born this way.
Despite your unlucky life that gave me mine,
I stand protected by the heather interconnected.
Purple flowers brush against my veins,
painting colors of potential growing pains.
I could blame you for festering these maniacal pests,
but I'm learning to sing through loving strains.

GENTLE RAGE

She holds close her gentle rage
and tears the name upon the page.
She calls on her blessed gods,
giving sacrifice for her odds.
Manifest her courage here,
watch her suffering disappear.
Adhere to her investing;
for now she has no fear.

NOT JUST THE MAN

In twilight's hush, a young love did reveal.
A maiden fair, in mystery's embrace.
Her heart enthralled by stories and appeal,
in every line, his silent strength she'd trace.

His eyes, like green aurora, were charming—
spoke worlds of burning fears and lost dreams.
His vulnerabilities were disarming,
she loved not just the man, but what he seems.

For passion, she learns, in loud silences ring.
Again, she loved not just the man, but the
potential that this love could bring.

SEA ME

And through the
night I stalked my ghost,
'til we stopped to
see the coast.

FLY ON THE WALL

In shadowed corners,
silent, hidden well;
a fly upon the wall,
with tales to tell.
In rooms where echoes
of the solitary abide,
it watches, unseen,
hidden in its pride.
The fly, with a faceted
and glistening eye,
beholds the secrets
that in stillness lie.
It sees the dance of dust
spirits in slanted light,
the creeping of the lady
from day to eerie night,
the ticking clock that beats
like a heart forlorn, or
the sighs that lead to
a wretched kind of mourn.
And in its wings,
holds integrity in its tone,
because the fly
knows what it's like
to live a life all alone.

SAVAGE

A girl with eyes of embers glow,
spits fire fierce against the flow.
Her gaze lights up with burning might,
she stands her ground, prepared to fight.
Compared to the others' diddly-squat,
she climbs her way through every plot.
Her wit as quick as the flames she strides,
she leaps beyond obstacles, surfing those tides.
And, despite the frailty of size and shape,
that girl is a savage yet the artist of her dreamscape.

I FORGIVE YOU

One last laugh bellowing;
one last hand squeeze and the following.
One last lesson wavering,
and one last embrace; uncovering.

Give me your hand and stand here with me.
Atop this mountain, we can dream by the sea.
Maybe then we can both feel free
from the burdens of those talking fountains.

THE NIGHT I FELL FOR YOU

I remember the dream I had the night I fell in love with you. I was traveling on a barren road until I glanced to the right and saw the vast ocean before me. Although the clouds were torn by incoming thunder, the ocean waved crystal blue. Spontaneously, I followed the calling toward the shore and found empty bottles half-buried in the sand. While the storm was approaching, the air was still. The hues mocked one another, moving from peach to a deep purple. I decided to jump in, though I did not hold my breath, for I wasn't afraid of being consumed. Serenity chose me that night, and I loved you harder the morning after.

DEFINE THEM

People are like words; always definable,
yet there's more to them than meets the eye.
Layers deep within—uncontainable;
as if the letters themselves could lie.

SHADOW SELF

I think about the parts of us that are concealed within the hollow cavities of our bones, calling for shadow work. They require listeners, and who better to listen to them than the bold parts of us gasping for change.

PRUDENT

I come to with a sense of renewal,
like the trees concurrently blooming in early spring.
And my body, although residing in the same space
from last winter, breathes differently; prolonging my thoughts.
I am in love with the cycles that reach me—
always knocking but never offering any formalities.
And my hands, despite cold fingers stained by consequence,
continue to write my story in prudent proximity to the
darkness that tries to shelter me.

FALTERING

Gripped by she
who knows not me.
In a memory,
too far to see.
Faltering dreams
sink to extremes,
yet those screams
under the seams
lie silently.

LANDESCAPE

The fawn across the trusted valley
stumbles in the grass,
as I watch, still, from afar.
A fawn so alone—
where is your mother?
For I ponder the question
cowering beneath my subconscious.

This empty landscape
where once she stood.
And I place this fawning stillness
before the yawn
that urges me to yell,
as if the selfish parts of me
cling to the mother deer
hiding in the trees.

PORES

Salt water pours,
from my salt water pores,
on a beach in the sand,
my mind is yours.

INTENT

Intentions are the only subjective measure of authenticity that describe a person's will in life. They are our innate objectives and most desired outcomes. Intentions are tricky to assess because they require a level of trust that saturates the space between what is felt and what is seen. Yet, they are simply understood as a relatable aspect of the human experience. The complexities that stir emotional reactivity cause unpredictable circumstances; however, intentions remain one of the few variables we can always control within ourselves. Many have "good" intentions because it is embedded in our nature to depend on the emotional collaboration of others. There is a balance to all things, however, and diversity can be a bitter pill to swallow during times of argument. Values, processes, and lifestyles are built on intention—or must be—in order to reach satisfaction in life. Thus, I say with certainty that differences in our ways of living do not point to negative intentions, but rather to our freedom to choose who we wish to become. If we do not like who we are, then a change is festering under the skin. It is then time to shed the processes and perspectives that no longer inspire intention.

MOTHER'S LESSON

To be a woman,
I've come to see,
is to give selflessly,
yet remain wholly me.

Loyalty deep
to family and kin,
but there's also a strength
to nurture within.

From daughter to mother:
a legacy to grow,
but along with tradition,
my own path must flow.

To love with each action;
to stand with grace,
yet etch out a space
that's mine to embrace.

You trusted my father
when life felt unclear,
so I trust my own voice,
as I follow you here.

MOTHS ARE ONLY TEMPORARY

Moths inhale the light and exhale the darkness. They represent the pursuit of knowledge, truth, and enlightenment amid life's uncertainties. As moths are drawn to natural luminescence, they search for clarity and understanding. Their brief existence is a metaphor for the transient nature of life, where moments of clarity flicker like fleeting thoughts. We must learn to embrace change and find balance in all things. Their persistence to be revealed mirrors the human experience of seeking purpose in a world full of ambiguity.

A moth's duality—the contrast between its attraction to the light and its origins in the dark—reflects the balance we must find between the known and the unknown, the certainty we crave, and the chaos we must learn to accept both in the world and within ourselves. I am guided by the wisdom of the moth. I have been led through the darkened parts of life's uncertainties toward the fleeting illuminations of truth. I have learned to embrace uncertainty rather than fear it. I am both shadow and glow, as I now possess a deeper acceptance of life's impermanent freedom to release the need to control all that I am and all that surrounds me.

I understand that life's inconsistencies are temporary as they continue to teach me the values of resilience, reflection, and rest.

TREAT ME

To treat me the way I crave
is not to conceal me in silk kisses,
but to push me when I feel I can't proceed;
to remind me that I desire a sensational life of depth;
to ignite our bond with stimulation to fortify this love.
Otherwise, you aren't treating me for who I truly am.
You are loving the version of me you wish to see.
I long for wonderous growth through every test,
to feel the assembly of emotional extremes,
to entertain myself in the pleasures of a
beautiful and worthy kind of love.
Challenge me, and I will love you
until the earth turns to dust.

DARK EMPATH

I feel the gaze; cold, calculated, friendly.
There is a clone who reads the rhythms of my guilt.
Behind the curtain, a dark empath sees me,
and guides themselves on what my heart has built.

With a genuine sense of knowing how I feel,
and a cognitive response to every move.
There lies a shadow whispering wounds that won't heal,
til' they become the darkness they must prove.

Yet read them well, and in them, grasp your fate,
for in this match, both sides begin to bleed.
I have created boundaries in such a cruel debate,
so, I say, water your mind's compassionate seed.

To heal that damage, to be worthy of a remark;
only a self-transparent love can remove you from the dark.

THE TEST

Abuse and negligence are two dark shadows that cast different kinds of harm at the silent intersections of perception and action. The deliberate and swift force of abuse leaves wounds that sting and fracture, striking a child's development with a sharp edge of intentionality. Negligence, by contrast, is a softer, colder presence—a silent failure to take responsibility and truly care for a child. Whether by an active hand or a passive voice, there is no turn in time that reverses the lived lessons endured by the innocent. Trauma is inevitable for children caught in the crossfire; however, healing can be both a potentiality and a constant. Children may grow and learn to understand the cards that have been dealt. Those of us who know what it's like to toss and turn through waves of uncertainty can approach our challenges as an opportunity to be better, or we can use the same perspectives that caused the trauma. Forgiveness is not always for them, but for the person you might grow up to be. Although maturity resides in the mercy you give in the face of old mistakes, adulthood provides the test. How will you approach the hypocrisies in yourself? Will you beat a statistic, or continue distressing the cycles that raised you?

THAT MAN

I love that man,
that man of mine.

I love that man,
'til the end of time.

I love that man,
because he is divine.

I love that man,
that makes me rhyme.

I love that man,
who treats me fair.

I love that man,
who does not dare.

I love that man,
his essence rare.

He loves me too,
I find.

MY FATHER'S INSTILLED WORDS

The shittiest thing to do to someone is to tell them that one of their natural gifts is a coping mechanism. If you have no dreams, you have no reality. We must be consistent in our approach. I'll lasso the moon and give the stars to every single one of you. We don't have to live life by a stereotype. Are you assuming my assumption? The meaning to life is contribution. At the end of the day, will you be the one to plug away and burn the midnight oil? Don't call me unless you need me; if I raised you right, you won't need to. Make your life extraordinary so that my life has meaning. You want me to stop talking? Then silence me with your actions. Insanity is becoming comfortable with the dysfunctional outcome. We don't judge; we forecast. I'm going to tell you something that'll shock the very foundation of who you think you are. Just prop me up in the corner with a hammer in my hand, and the house will get built. We have it quoted already and stenciled in stone. There is no privilege to rebellion, only restriction. I'm not going to pretend that I'm the wisest in the room; I'm going to claim it. The only balance that exists is the balance we allow. I'm intrigued by the potential of you. I save her in my dreams. Draw what you see, not what you think you see. If you do what you've always done, you'll get what you've always gotten. You're my grace; my second chance.

PSYCHO

We've all felt the edges of madness;
to dissect our thoughts,
to separate who we think we are
from how the world perceives us.
We've all been caught in the cycle
of obsessing over the moments
that make us question our actions;
to defend our emotions fiercely,
believing we are justified;
to reach into the unsteady corners of
ourselves and let our raw humanity show.

We've all wandered through the asylum
hidden under the shadows of our minds.
And if you haven't—
gaze into your reflection a little longer,
and tell me what looks back at you.

BAGGAGE

Please don't search for the
space between my words;
absent of clarification.
So that you can drop your luggage,
and plant your seeds,
and unpack all of your baggage.

VERACITY

I think I'm giving my last breath
to ears made of clay, deaf to my veracity.
If this is who you choose to be,
why complain about the imposter residing in you?
What secrets do you hide from yourself?
Who did you flee from that has led you here?

Story of my life; a dreamer with a heart that
misinterprets the collateral of original thought.
And though I've grown into a listener,
if no one hears my words,
then what remains of me?

TAKE THE RISK

You're anxious about beginning again,
worried that mistakes may
leave a lasting mark;
nervous of the shifts needed
to grow into a better self.

Take the leap, seize the opportunity—
it's all in how you view yourself.
You must choose to grow
or you'll remain in the stagnancy
of a life that no longer serves you.

What causes more damage to your spirit:
the irritability of living the same way,
or a potential threat to your routine?
Uncertainty can be numbing to the
parallels we build within our character.

Your capacities are honest and strong,
and you are worthy of beautiful things.
Take the risk. Welcome the change.
Pursue a life that serves you
instead of one that confines you.

PACIFIC NORTHWEST

The city isn’t meant for me;
where carbon towers rise,
drying flowers 'neath the skies,
and clouds are choked by debris.

Pacific Northwest, my home;
where natural towns abide.
A playground far and wide
for those like me who seek to roam.

So, I’ll live out my dream
among the ever steep trees,
where I can breathe with ease,
and light within the mist will gleam.

OVERWATER

When things are too organized,
We tend to burden ourselves with expectation.
It's okay to grow beyond yesterday, but
overwatering won't make us flourish faster.
Don't wilt your dreams with oversaturated goals.
You deserve to breathe in sunlight, free from obligation.

SPILLING

Spilling over things that remain unworded
while hinged memories treat our traumas.
Why must these children who whimper at
the sound of tumultuous noises suffer
in the aftermath of supposed healing?
That minute lasted a second too long.
She spoke riddles to me: that girl who
was raised with contradicting lessons.
Unlearning the wordless is a challenge
we all must face time and time again.
When I give birth to a child of the earth,
I will say the words quietly without spilling.

DEEPEST ENTIRETY

To endure the test of time
we must ask ourselves:
"If we cannot today, then what
makes us think we can tomorrow?"
Do not nod at this, for it takes words
to express our deepest entirety.
We all have a story to tell,
yet not everyone folds under commentary.
We must learn to answer this question,
not only for our intentions, but for the parts
of us who desire to show up for the world.
Observe the clues,
search for the epiphany,
and listen to the ideas that drift toward you.
A shifting narrative is step one in
deciding to trust the process.

MILESTONES OF SELF-HONESTY

Establishing and maintaining boundaries.
Prioritizing self-care and your own needs.
Shifting from extreme thinking to nuanced thinking.
Ending a toxic relationship or beginning a healthy one.
Cultivating compassion and purpose in your daily life.
Decreasing the rate of negative self-talk.
Feeling proud of yourself while learning to manage anxieties.
Providing yourself with more options.
Alleviating stress, anxiety, and depression.
Reducing the risk of hereditary mood disorders.
Attracting honest and authentic people.
Building trust, reliability, and autonomy in your character.
Reaching goals that you set for yourself.
Being you.

METAMORPHOSIS

Change is essential in our lives;
a quiet current beneath the surface,
where once I flinched
like a moth toward flame,
now I pause, breathe, and wait.
I used to let emotions crash over me,
like a relentless tide pulling me under.
But now I see a rhythm in the way
we rise, drift, and transform.

There are times we surrender and
let the sea carry us where it must.
And sometimes that opens our mind,
like the wings of a moth.
I have learned that strength
lies not in resistance,
but in the release of knowing
when to drift with the tide,
and when to swim against it.

I will not let the undertow claim my mind,
nor will I let fear set the course.
There is power in stillness;
in the steady, deliberate breath—
and in the calm between the storms.

(continued)

(continued)

Emotions, mindsets, and intentions
now flow together in depth.
Each choice has meaning.
Each step is aligned.
Consistency is no longer a weight,
but a promise I've made to myself.
As long as I continue to
lay the groundwork, brick by brick.
I feel an anchor within that stabilizes
me through the waves of change.
I have shed the cocoon of reaction,
carried the light of reflection,
and in this metamorphosis,
I find not the end of uncertainty,
but the beginning of resilience.

KILL THEM

There's only so many times you can kill
with kindness before it turns on you.
Many have wielded kindness like a weapon—
to appear empathetic, to maintain calm
in the storm, to bridge gaps of understanding,
to soothe tensions and salvage a bond with grace.

But for those who prey on this softness,
kindness becomes an open wound to exploit,
draining you until nothing remains but what
serves those who lack the emotional depth
to see the value of your boundaries.
In killing them with kindness,
I hold myself captive;
bound by the chains of a smile
too honest to break free from.

DWELLER

To stand
in the silhouette of a tree
is to be one with our nature,
shielded by the sun—
a reflection
of the shaded parts of humanity.

Do we hide
from the light
of the knowing,
or are we merely dwellers
in the comfort of our shadows?

TRUST THE JOURNEY

To withstand the challenges we face
and grow into who we are meant to be,
we may reach ourselves by looking within
to assess our strengths and our motivations.
We may question the hold of procrastination
during the nonchalant cries for effortless change.

Wisdom alone isn't enough—we may engage
with reflections to reveal our other halves.
Stand firm in the narrative of honesty;
not everyone bends beneath criticism.
Learn to answer the hard questions,
not for appearances, but to align
with our most practical desires.
To show up authentically,
we may need to trust
the journey.

UNTAPPED

The world
is in need of you.

There's an untapped market
craving your perspectives,
your actions, your words,
and your laughter.

You hold something powerful—
a version of you
no one has ever seen.

In this life,
we are in shortage of authenticity.
Peer within, find something akin,
and dive into your untapped potential.

PRACTICE AND PATIENCE

The clunking of a relationship
as traditions drift and settle.
You may tremble under the weight
of patience stretched thin, pulled tight.
It's okay to stand alone, even when sharing space;
to escape the confines of your mind
in moments of stillness between you.
This doesn't lessen what exists between lovers—
instead, appreciation deepens in quiet conversations,
in the shared presence that asks for nothing in return.
Romantic love calls for a level of self-love,
one that grows slowly, nourished by practice and patience.

ETHOS

Our society is soaked by ethos;
a spiraling mix of temperament and individualism,
where each belief forms like a weather system.
We stride through storms we don't understand,
feel winds of opinions shaping all that is around us.
Yet, here we are—
still waiting for our own narratives to drizzle
like light rain on the sills of our thoughts.

The years stack like stones,
a monument to the time spent not choosing,
not becoming the characters
we thought we would be by now.

But this is simply the consequence of autonomy.
We teach others how to treat us
without even knowing we are teachers.
Sometimes we don't even teach ourselves.
A glance toward evolution, a word, or nothing at all—
nonetheless, we reflect the patterns drawn in thin air.

In the end, we are both the storm and the stillness,
shaped by the ethos and yet,
we pick up the characters we hope to shape within ourselves.

TO BUILD VALUE

Eat consciously.
Make movement a daily habit.
Sleep for at least 7 hours a night.
Maintain a fairly consistent AM and PM routine.
Stimulate your thinking.
Actively learn new skills.
Challenge your ideas with intention.
Practice creative reading and writing.
Cope with your stressors.
Find an outlet to reflect on life.
Build self-awareness through empathy.
Connect with nature.
Declutter your personal spaces.
Respect the places others reside in.
Stick to financial goals.
Avoid impulse-spending.
Invest in a savings plan.
Communicate transparently.
Craft authentic relationships.
Build purpose through a moral code.
Engage in ritual practice or prayer.
Set intentions and analyze your beliefs.
Seek a healthy work-life balance.
Assess your job satisfaction quarterly.
Aim for continuous self-development.
Know when to rest.

CAN OF WORMS

Open up a can of worms with me,
and we can toss them into the sea.
Those vineyard walks and late-night talks
taught me who I needed to be.

And this day in the sun,
which those moments had wrung,
led me to believe there's more to me.
From values mid-torn and morality worn,
I realize I had the key to be free.

I was saved as a child,
though stayed loud and wild,
despite anxieties urging me to flee.
So I say with trust,
to love is a must,
when opening a can of worms by the sea.

WE ARE IN A BATTLE BETWEEN

transformation / tradition
consistency / contradiction
healing / suffering
solace / connection
chaos / structure
stagnancy / change
indulgence / discipline
ambition / complacency
empathy / egotism
resilience / fragility
affirmation / rejection
explanation / silence
anxiety / serenity
stillness / transition
moderation / gluttony
creativity / conformity
reflection / impulsivity
abandonment / commitment
flexibility / rigidity
learning / ignorance
generosity / malevolence
denial / transparency
mindfulness / distraction

ILLUMINATE ME

I'm left in a state of exposure.
My composure still as the light flickers.
Moths uncover, like peeling stickers.

Illuminate me.
Free from the dark of night, shielding.
This luminosity is my own, unyielding.

Persistence of vision, muttering.
Fluttering shadows trace the bright space.
The moths have left me with lingering grace.

Is this a lucid dream?
Themes of illumination paint a sanctuary.
Remember now, the moths are only temporary.

To live a life without dysfunction means you must prioritize resilience, reflection, and rest.

Uncertainties exist.

How you approach change is crucial
to the ebb and flow of your journey.

Hannah Grace Spenner is a poet, writer, and content strategist based in the Pacific Northwest. Dedicated to child advocacy, she pursues a career in nonprofit communications. Alongside her professional endeavors, Hannah is passionate about creative writing, wicca, and wellness. Hannah's core aspiration is to foster growth, mindfulness, and balance through her contributions.

Thank you for joining me on this journey through my words. Stay connected for more insights, stories, and updates.

Find me on Instagram:
@h.grace.s

Explore more at:
hgraces.com

For inquiries, reach me at:
hannah.spenner@gmail.com

ISBN: 979-8-218-98669-8 (2nd Edition, 2024)
ISBN: 979-8-8720-9859-1 (1st Edition, 2023)

Book design by Hannah Grace Spenner
Printed in the United States of America.

Independently Published by H.GRACE.S

www.ingramcontent.com/pod-product-compliance
Lightning Source LLC
La Vergne TN
LVHW041250080426
835510LV00009B/671
* 9 7 9 8 2 1 8 9 8 6 6 9 8 *